THE IDLER GUIDE TO ANCIENT PHILOSOPHY

THE IDLER GUIDE TO

ANCIENT PHILOSOPHY

Dr. Mark Vernon

IDLER PRESS

MMXVI

Published by Idler Press
Unit 7 Great Western Studios 65 Alfred Road London W2 5EU

ISBN 978-0-9548456-6-7

Pattern design by Alice Smith

Typesetting by Bracketpress

Fourth Edition

www.idler.co.uk

Ancient *adjective* \ˈān(t)-shənt, ˈāŋ(k)-shənt\
Existing for many years, Greco-Roman, perennial

Philosophy *noun* \fə-ˈlä-s(ə-)fē\
From Greek, *philia* – to love, befriend, desire for something possessed in part; and *sophia* – wisdom, a practical, emotional, intellectual and spiritual capability

Contents

I.

The Prequel: Presocratics

Our story begins a long time ago in a universe that, psychologically speaking, is pretty far away. It is the age of Homer – of warriors and heroes, gods and monsters. Oral means of communication were the norm, not writing: thoughts were written on the heart before they were transferred to the page. An individual in those times – the undifferentiated years of the tenth, ninth, eighth centuries BC – might have looked at the red sky, the black sea or the green land (ancient Greeks had no word for blue) and felt a flood of meaning washing from the hills and waves. The experience was unlike a modern mentality in which we spontaneously turn inside seeking insight in introspection.

There was, as yet, no clear distinction between inside and outside yourself. Human beings were porous, as the philosopher Charles Taylor has put it. Hence, if you read Homer, you find that his heroes have crises but unlike Shakespeare's Hamlet, they do not stand on an empty stage and reflect via soliloquy. 'To be or not to be ... ' Such deliberation requires a sense of self that is individual, separate, facing its own unique clusters of pain. Rather, in Homer, a miasma rises up, the scene cuts to gods arguing on Olympus, and the characters of Achilles or Hecuba are played like chess pieces in the game called fate. They have what the philologist Owen Barfield called participatory consciousness. We are therefore I am, not I think therefore I am.

Things began to shift in the first stirrings of what we now call philosophy. The presocratic philosophers were those individuals who began to ask the kind of questions that cause a certain distance to open between the individual and the world in which they had felt immersed. They began to create a mentality that feels more familiar to us, one that planted the seeds of the modern. We know one of those queries left by Anaxamines of Miletus, one of the earliest philosophers of the sixth century. He thought to blow on his hand in two ways. First, with his mouth wide open. Then, with his lips pursed. He noticed a difference. Try it.

When blowing with his mouth wide open, the air felt warm. With his lips pursed, it felt cold on his hand. And then he thought to ask why?

That small question represents a massive leap of mind. It wonders if the difference might have a physical reason, a proto-scientific explanation. We now describe the effect as a result of Boyle's law. The air from pursed lips feels cooler because it undergoes a rapid expansion as it leaves your mouth. That takes energy, so the temperature drops. The air from an open mouth undergoes no change of pressure, and so emerges still warm, at body temperature.

But there is something more subtle going on in Anaxamines' 'why' too. The effect of asking is to distance you from the experience itself. Part of you has the experience of warm and cool air hitting your palm. But now, another part of you takes an inner step back and reflects on the experience. That inner shift is symptomatic of the new way of engaging with life that was emerging at the time of the presocratics. It is that change of consciousness they can be said to have helped crystalize. It is as if alongside life known as a series of fateful events, a deeper truth may be found by turning inwards and reflecting. Introspection had begun.

It carries benefits and costs. One big benefit is that sciences can get going. The presocratics are remembered for coming up with questions we still ask, such as what the world is made of, can I predict whether it will rain tomorrow, do living organisms evolve? Their answers, like ours, also made them more capable of manipulating the world. The change put power in their hands. Another early philosopher, Thales also of Miletus, was such an astute observer of nature that he was able to forecast that next summer would be particularly good for olives. His new science gave him the confidence to buy the rights to license olive presses. Next summer came and he made a killing, because he was correct. Everyone had to pay him a small tax to capitalise on the bumper crop.

But there is a cost of prioritising this more analytical, manipulative form of consciousness over a participatory one, too. It is separation. Hence, Barfield labeled this new phase of life, alienated. I now have the sense that there is a distance between myself and the world, one that feels difficult to bridge because I regard myself as an isolated subject, an 'I', in a universe of objects, or things. The shift from an oral to a written culture has a similar effect. Put words on a page, and you cause the illusion that they have an abstract, virtual existence; no longer living in the heart but on the page. What they describe need not be intimately tied to our experience. Hence we know Hamlet as an artifice, a fiction. Homer's hearers must have felt his heroes existed, in some archetypal way. Similarly, we no longer live with the supposition of oral cultures who see words in the landscape, aboriginal meanings in the stars and clouds. Hereon, philosophy runs the risk of seeming to conquer all mysteries 'by rule and line', to recall Keats' lament for those lost times.

The effects of these changes in the presocratic era have evolved over the centuries, responding to socio-economic as well as ideological developments. For example, whilst Thales thought to capitalise on his new knowledge, it was not until the early modern period of the seventeenth and eighteenth centuries that science and technology became the *raison d'être* of entire societies, in the industrial revolutions. Alternatively, it was the conditions of the nineteenth century that generated a new kind of human being, the atheist, who concluded there was a fundamental gulf between the worldview known as scientific and that known as religious. An ancient philosopher, upon making a discovery, would have thought it entirely sensible and appropriate to offer a sacrifice in the local temple. 'Everything is full of gods,' Thales the meteorologist also delighted in declaring.

None of the ancient philosophers felt it necessary to ask whether there was a meaning to life either. If anything, they struggled because life was too full of meaning. They did not adopt the assumption that disconnected introspection alone must adjudication on purpose and fulfillment. That took the emergence of an ideal of self-sufficient, self-determining, autonomous individuality. Ancient philosophers, like most humans in history, argued that asking *where* you are is as valuable a question as asking *who* you are: they followed the injunction to *know thyself* rather than the more modern need to *make* something of oneself.

But nonetheless, the assumptions that shape us now find an early reflection in the surviving fragments of works by individuals like Anaxamines and Thales. Unlike Homer, who always comes across as a bit dreamy and mythological, their inquiries feel familiar. Their take on life is striking because, though two and a half thousand years old, it feels related to our own.

Let us be a little more specific and highlight three further presocratics whose insights have proven particularly long-lived and powerful: Pythagoras, Heraclitus and Parmenides. They and their followers first were active in the last 50 years of the sixth century BC, that is, a generation or so before Socrates was born.

Pythagoras is so important because it was he, or his disciples, who became fascinated by the links between mathematics, nature and music. The story goes that Pythagoras passed by a blacksmiths' one day. He noticed that when the smithy halved the length of an iron bar and hit it again, the note that sounded leapt up an octave. Different proportionate adjustments to bar length produced other harmonious tones. The conclusion was that mathematics is written into the fabric of nature, and moreover in such a way as to be aesthetically beautiful. That is astonishing, even magical, and led the Pythagoreans to conclude that the cosmos is an enchanting, patterned place.

That there should be a relationship between abstract numbers and the movement of the stars, or the growth of populations, or shifts in climate, can be thought humdrum today. Galileo himself was once heard to exclaim, we are all Pythagoreans now. But when you next hear a scientist or mathematician describe a solution as compelling because it is simple, or elegant, or generative, or universal, you are hearing the echoes of the ancient Pythagoreans whose philosophy revitalized an older sense of mystery.

Heraclitus, a second presocratic who was particularly important in this age, was the master of the aphorism. Luckily for us, many of his pithy and paradoxical sayings survive. 'You can't step into the same river twice.' 'The road up and down is one and the same.' 'The sea – he says – water most pure and most impure; for fishes drinkable and healthy; for humans undrinkable and deadly.' He invites his followers to read his sayings, wrestle with their meaning, and so discover insights for themselves.

One of his central fixations was that everything is in a state of flux and change, oscillating between opposites like day and night, love and hate, ordered and chaotic. He likened the world to a drink of the time that was a bit like a vinaigrette. A vinaigrette stays what it is because the wine and vinegar are kept in motion. If that stops and the ingredients settle, the dressing ceases to exist. Heraclitus felt that such disturbances permeated the cosmos and were not to be lamented because they are the source of all creativity.

Again, it was an idea with legs. The great nineteenth century philosophers Hegel and Marx agreed. Inherent in any thesis is its antithesis, Hegel argued, which propels history forward to a new synthesis. Marx made the dynamic the basis of his economic theory: the contradictions generated by the turbulence that is part of capitalism leads to its breakdown and the emergence of a new dispensation: communism. Late capitalist cultures still assesses their health by the rate of change and development called economic growth; the process of progress is known as creative destruction. We are all Heracliteans now too.

Third, there's Parmenides. Apart from anything else, he is significant because he trusted reason. It was another relatively new idea and not an obvious one. Even today, we can struggle with it because reason often tells us things that we don't want to accept. Stop smoking, drive carefully, chose wisely in love, work less.

Parmenides trusted reason and felt that it led him to a radical, profoundly counterintuitive conclusion. Everything is singular, unchanging, unified. He knew that his experience insisted the world was multiple, changeable, conflicted. He had been young and was now old. There had been wine in the cellar and now there was not. It had been day but now he could see the stars shining through the windows of his temple-home in Elea, southern Italy. But reason told him that such perceptions were deluded. And he must trust that. Why?

The nub of reason's argument is that something cannot come out of nothing. The book in your hand did not spring, spontaneously into existence. An author wrote it, a printer manufactured it, a bookseller purveyed it. We live in a universe, the extraordinary product of a primordial Big Bang, the standard model of physics tells us. But the Big Bang itself depended upon something that was not nothing – the quantum vacuum whose random fluctuations possibly produced it.

That much perhaps makes sense. The cosmos does not serve up free lunches. But Parmenides felt that reason pushes the logic a step further, to a conclusion that is almost impossible to accept. He argued that reason also tells us there is no such thing as change, because change implies that something is now that wasn't before. And this is just another version of the false claim that something can spring out of nothing.

In fact, he noticed, you can't even talk about nothing – 'nothing' being a compound word that is no more than a negation: no-thing. So it is not only that something cannot come from nothing, and therefore there can be no real change, but that nothing is not even a real concept in itself. 'Being is indestructible, whole, of one kind, unwavering and complete,' Parmenides averred in one of the two surviving poems expounding his position.

This reliance on reason over experience – and the conclusion that appearances massively deceive – has led to him being called the father of metaphysics, and again science and the modern worldview owes much to a similar insistence. The book in your hand feels solid, but quantum physics tells you the pages are knots of immaterial electro-magnetic fluctuations misleadingly called matter. Einstein found such insights a comfort when contemplating his presumed mortality. 'Life and death flow into one, and there is neither evolution nor destiny; only being.' He was being thoroughly Parmenidean.

We do the presocratics a disservice, I fear, in rattling through a few of their thoughts in a handful of the things we call pages. But perhaps you would like to pursue one or more of these figures elsewhere, particularly if you feel Pythagorean, Heraclitean or Parmenidean about life. In our short introduction, we must push on, and come now to the defining figure of the western philosophical tradition. It may seem unfair or arbitrary to call the philosophers before him, 'presocratics', as if they missed the main event. It is, in a way. They did not know what was to follow. They are striking, consciousness-shifting philosophers in their own right. But there is a logic to this division in our story. If the presocratics set the stage, Socrates stepped onto it.

2.

Why Socrates? Why the hemlock?

You know in depth about Socrates already, though it may not feel like that. You may recall the year in which he died, 399 BC; or that he was condemned to death and drank hemlock; or that he invented a technique called Socratic questioning; or that he thought the unexamined life was not worth living. But a scattering of facts aside, it may feel that you know little more. But you do.

One of the reasons why he is the standout figure in western philosophy is that he is inside the heads of us all. We do not just agree with some of his idea, as we do with Pythagoras and Heraclitus and Parmenides. Neither is it what he discovered that makes a difference, like a set of scientific laws. It was his spirit, something about his very person, that got under people's skin – an energy unleashed first on ancient Athens that then spread around the world. Learn something more about Socrates and how he lived and you learn something more about your own life, psyche and soul.

He is one of those rare characters in history who wrote nothing in his own hand, was rejected by his home town, and was thought by many to be a failure in his own time, and yet changed everything. Alongside Socrates, can be placed the Buddha, Confucius and Jesus. They have been called axial figures by the German philosopher, Karl Jaspers, by which is meant lives on which the wheels of civilisations were subsequently seen to have definitively turned. Like those other religious figures, an encounter with Socrates leaves nothing feeling quite the same again.

And I think it is useful to think of him as a religious figure, more than a rational thinker or moral hero or political victim, though he can be said to be those things too. By religious I don't mean that he taught doctrinal truths. He actually claimed to know nothing for sure. Or that he insisted on the worship of gods, though he felt he was called by Apollo. Rather, he is a religious figure because to meet him is to have the constellation of your mind re-organised, in a way that you didn't expect, but feels revelatory.

But how do we meet him now, at the beginning of the twenty-first century? Well, here's an exercise you might like to try with a partner or friend. Chose someone carefully because it can be quite a disturbing assignment to fulfill.

Take turns repeatedly to ask each other a very simple question. 'Who are you?' So, say you start. You ask your friend: who are you, who are you, who are you? They offer short replies each time: Emma, a vicar, a mother. Then after a minute or so, you swap. Who are you, who are you, who are you? Mark, a former-vicar, a cat lover.

When you've done that for a minute or so each, move onto a second task. Ask yourselves what it was like to do the exercise.

When I've run this in groups, individuals almost always say that it was difficult. They are left feeling unsettled, aware of how aggressive such pithy questioning can be, and/or illuminated by the realisation that straightforward questions can be so tough to answer. In that experience, you gain a sense of what it must have been like to meet Socrates.

According to Plato, and other sources, he spent much of the second half of his life hanging around the central marketplace in Athens asking basic stuff of those he encountered. It seems likely that his inquiries included: what is friendship, what is justice, what is courage, what is love? – the everyday matters that we take for granted, and which Plato has Socrates pursue in the dialogues he subsequently wrote about his teacher, of which around 30 survive. Socrates' main point seems to have been that we actually know least about what we assume we know most about. Who are you? It is shockingly hard to say.

This is an existential view of Socrates, and not one that you're likely to encounter in modern philosophy departments. There, it is his rationality that is celebrated. I have heard him introduced as 'the man who sought definitions'. But is that reason enough to kill the man, as the ancient Athenians did? Does that explain why everyone has heard of him, though many feel they know little about him?

The trouble is that university life today has so little to do with philosophical life back then. You don't secure tenure, become a professor, or score well in the Research Assessment Exercise by caring for your soul, which is what Plato felt Socrates did supremely well. You win academic prizes by undermining the proposals of competitor colleagues.

Hence, professional journals on Socrates are stuffed with articles asking what Socrates believed, what Plato's portrayal of Socrates has to do with the historical Socrates (the so-called Socratic problem), or even whether Socrates existed at all – though thankfully the fashion for asking that one has abated in recent years. This is all a reflection of the sad fact that academics today are massively pressured to ask questions because it aids their career, not because they might live better.

This is not just to take a cheap shot at academic life. It is also to make a vital philosophical point. Plato's efforts in writing his dialogues were aimed at capturing the spirit of what it was like to encounter Socrates. They are certainly not supposed to be records of actual exchanges. Plato knew that a drama, not a history, would be more valuable to subsequent generations, like us. Now, we too can gain from his spirit, can make something more of lives with their different sets of constraints and conditions.

To put it another way, Plato wrote dialogues – and we know he only wrote dialogues conveying characters with hearts as well as minds, with desires as well as logic – because he knew that philosophy dies when reduced to an argument about words. He wanted to grip us as a whole person. He is more interested in our practice than our theories. Plato and Socrates must sigh every time a student sits a philosophy exam. The examination they strove to nurture was of one's life, not of one's cleverness – another reason why it is better to think of Socrates as a religious figure, not a professor. You did not learn from Socrates by taking notes or memorising the facts of his life. His students – then and now – imbibe his curiosity, introject his inner freedom, feed on the love of life that his life radiated. He must have been an amazing teacher.

I've made my point. But a little history can be helpful too. Socrates first came to the attention of the public not as a guru but as a warrior. For much of his life, Athens was at war. He was commended for his bravery, having on occasion risked his life to save the lives of others. He was also remarked upon for his oddities. If you asked an ancient Athenian about Socrates, they might well have replied that he wore no shoes, or had a habit of standing stock still for several hours, not that he was a clever-clogs.

But perhaps it was because he was odd, and so challenged the conventions of his times, that some also asked what his peculiarities were about? Like an ancient Mediterranean version of Mahatma Gandhi, columnists and commentators would wrestle with whether his habits and utterances were meaningful or empty, should be explored or ignored?

The story goes that an impetuous and longstanding friend of

Socrates, Chaerephon, decided the case needed to be settled. So he set off to consult the oracle at Delphi. He made the trip from Athens, a few day's journey on foot. He threw the water over the goat, and the creature shuddered. He stood before the temple of Apollo, and gazed up at the words inscribed on the portico: *Know Thyself!* He was admitted to the inner sanctum, perhaps crossing a priest's palm with silver. And finally stood before the Pythia, the prophetess who spoke the words of the god and, incidentally, probably did not inhale hallucinogenic vapours, as is sometimes said today. The latest research suggests the rocks on which the temple stands could not have admitted such aids to spiritual experience. And she delivered her message. 'No-one is wiser than he,' she said.

We might imagine Chaerephon rushing back home delighted. What an endorsement for his friend! But Socrates was wary, and wise. He knew that oracles need to be tested. The messages they deliver are not literal. The truth lies beneath the words. They must be discerned. Oracles were such valuable and successful institutions in the ancient world not because they straightforwardly told individuals what was coming but because they helped them struggle with the vicissitudes of life and so make something of the future for themselves.

Socrates decided he must try to find someone who was wiser than he, and so prove the oracle wrong. First, he asked the politicians of the young democracy, those who sought support from citizens by telling them they knew how to govern a city-state, win its wars, preserve its good life. That must mean they were wise on what a good life is. Except, it turned out they weren't. Worse, they believed their own flawed rhetoric.

Socrates turned to the poets of his day. He presumably knew some of the best in history because he was a contemporary of the playwrights Aristophanes, Euripides and Sophocles. They were smart with words, it was true. They could pun and portray, move and manipulate an audience. But it was also the case, they admitted, that though words were their means, the results often conveyed way more than they realised. So there again was a group of people who looked wise, but whose wisdom had strict limitations.

Finally, he talked with the artisans – the skilled craftsmen who knew how to make shoes, and weapons, and pots. They were wise in these matters, having an intuitive, felt ability to work the materials of their trade. But perhaps they were like the proverbial London taxi-driver. He knows how to get you home and takes that as an excuse to offer you an opinion on the kindness of Margaret Thatcher or the birth certificate of Barack Obama. Not wise.

And then Socrates got it. It was not that he knew stuff. He too was unsure about the good life, about what words mean, about the limitations of knowing a craft. (He had been an apprentice stonemason in his early life.) But at least he knew that much. So he concluded, my wisdom such as it is, lies in knowing the bounds of my knowledge. One thing I know I know for sure, he is reported to have repeated: I know nothing for sure.

He then spent the rest of his life championing that insight. We are the creatures who are not just ignorant about many things, but can become cognisant of our ignorance. That awareness is invaluable and our great challenge. My cats, for example, are simply ignorant about where cat food comes from. They do not worry about it, unable to fall asleep on their mats. In general, no other creature, so far as we know, is haunted by doubt, uncertainty, the future. Integral to the human condition is frustration, consciousness of finitude, and not just physical pain but psychological suffering.

But there is an upside too, because lack also makes for fulfillment, creativity and invention, and not just the satisfaction of brute instincts but the joys of relationships and love. Civilisation itself is the product. We are the in-between animal, as Plato put it – finite and mortal, though also born with a taste for the infinite and eternal. Or as the Christian theologian, Augustine of Hippo, later poetically glossed the observation, human beings are between the beasts and angels. In the sciences, the arts and religion we reach for more, to transcend our limitations.

That was what it was like to meet Socrates. You felt this predicament clearly, you knew it in your guts. For many, the downsides were too much. Suddenly not knowing quite who you were caused them to fight Socrates or flee from him. There are reports that to hear Socrates was like being stung by a ray or bitten by a horse-fly. Others saw him coming along the narrow streets of Athens and snuck down a side alley. The nineteenth century admirer of Socrates, Søren Kierkegaard, noted that because human beings are both beast and angel, they are also the animal defined by anxiety. Many want answers not better questions. In 399BC, decades of animosity amongst the Athenians came to a head. Socrates was charged with introducing new gods to the city and corrupting the youth. Both were treasonable offences in times of war and upheaval – introducing new gods being a bit like declaring the enemy state sovereign; corrupting youth meaning encouraging the next generation to wonder whether the city's political leaders had it all wrong. He was found guilty and then sentenced to death. He elected execution by ingestion of hemlock, a more gentle exit than the alternative, crucifixion.

But a few could stomach the challenge. They made grappling with the human condition, as Socrates had revealed it, their life's work. They realised that his type of philosophy was an invitation not a set of instructions, a kind of showing not telling. That's why Socrates is a pivotal figure. That's why we know a lot about him, if we care to inspect our experience. And that's why engaging with his legacy promises more than just robust arguments or thorough definitions. It promises the difficult thing that another axial figure summed up as 'life in all its fullness'. Not everyone wants that: there is a shadow. Followers of Socrates do.

3.

Plato, Scepticism, and the God of Love

What is love? What is friendship? Is there any justice in the world, or is might right? How was the world made? Are circles perfect? Am I ever fully awake? The rest of ancient Greek philosophy can be thought of as a variety of responses to Socrates. And first we must say more about Plato – not least because if questions like these are some of yours, he offers copious food for thought.

The story goes that Plato was headed for the Dionysian festival, the great Athenian competition for playwrights. In an age of great poets, he had a possibly winning composition in his hand. But on the way, he met Socrates. Immediately, he turned from his life as a writer and adopted a new one as the philosopher's disciple. In his twenties then, he stayed with Socrates until his guru's death, and then set up the Academy, a philosophical community that met in a grove or park just outside the city walls. Statesmen and mathematicians, noble women and leisured slaves came to hear and converse with him. Then, in time, he penned his dialogues to spread the way of life around the Greek-speaking world. It is these texts that provide us with the richest picture of Socrates the man, and unlike other contemporary witnesses, one that makes sense of why Socrates came to be perceived as such an enemy and threat that he was finally condemned.

Plato had a long life too, and also made mistakes, not least when he become embroiled in a disastrous expedition to Sicily and the city of Syracuse. He was imprisoned and nearly lost his life to slavery or worse. But he got one thing quite right.

If there were a central issue around which his response to Socrates revolves, his best attempt to pick up the existential challenge Socrates' life conveyed, it would be the theme of love. One of the ways he defined love was as the desire for what you lack – the point being that you don't desire what you don't know at all, but only what you have glimpsed, what eludes you, what promises much, but you don't know fully and so long to do so. Anyone who has fallen in love knows as much: your only thought is how to be with your beloved more.

Hence, Plato thought, what exposure to Socrates really provokes is the realisation that our greatest task, individually and collectively, is to manage our ignorance and not be fooled by our yearnings. We can know what we know. We can know some of what we don't know. But what about the things we don't know we don't know? And worse, the things we do know, and prefer to pretend we don't? Loosen some of those knots and a creative life of material, philosophical and spiritual discovery unfolds around you. Tighten them and the desire for more that pulses through you might throttle you in jealousy, frustration and hate.

Plato was a great inventor of myths, the myth of the lost city of Atlantis being one of his best known. They capture the drama and reflect the magnitude of life's multitudinous potentials. Another, in his dialogue the *Symposium*, concerns the conception of Eros, the personified god of this passionate, desiring love. It begins with a party in heaven, thrown when Aphrodite was born. Poros, the god of resourcefulness, attended. He was the son of Metis, the god of cunning, and during the evening he became drunk on nectar. He fell asleep in Zeus' garden. Whilst snoozing, he was spotted by Penia, the god of poverty. Always longing to fill her inner emptiness, she had the idea that a child by Poros might do the trick. So she took her chance and made love. Eros was the result, and hence love was born a combination of lack, resourcefulness and cunning. When you are in love, possessed by the god, these are the feelings you know. With such a powerful god inside you, Plato implies, how to live well is indeed a pressing question.

His reply is conveyed in his dialogues. It is here that he develops the stance often called Socratic questioning, or the 'elenchus' meaning testing, though I think that is a misleading term. It suggests Plato treated life as an intellectual puzzle like solving the ultimate Sudoku. Reasoning is an important tool, he doubtless agreed. But reason cannot lift itself up by its own bootstraps. It is one of the capacities that can serve us in the responses we make to the deeper dynamic that runs through life, this unruly, yearning or pull that would make or break us. Plato's wisdom is about responding skillfully to the energy within us called love.

He sought to educate his own and his followers' hearts. One way to understand his approach is to recall an image he frequently deploys for Socrates, as midwife. A midwife helps others to give birth to the life that is inside them, safely on the one hand and on the other hand so that the new life might flourish. In a nutshell, this is what Platonic philosophy offers. Plato's dialogues show Socrates, Plato's model teacher, doing just that.

How he did so was by engaging with individuals in the state that he found them. Socrates, and so presumably Plato, seems to have had a powerful ability to detect where individuals were at and help them appropriately. One day, according to the dialogue called the *Lysis*, Plato has Socrates bumping into a fellow called Hippothales. The poor fellow was suffering from a wild infatuation with a statuesque youth called Lysis. He was blushing and bumbling and humming quiet, crazy songs to his beloved. Socrates immediately realised that there was little he could do for him in such a state. Not infrequently, in fact Plato portrays

Socrates as not afraid to tell individuals that first they need to live a little, suffer a little, make mistakes, feel their vulnerability – and then come back to him. That is the first stage in a Platonic education. You then have material to work on.

Those who have such baggage and are more aware of it – more able to reflect on their experience – he engaged further. Step away from what you think you know, Plato's dialogues imply, and move more into the unknown or hidden aspects of your life, expansive and frightening though that can be. This process is a generator of insight and wisdom.

It is a bit like the parent who helps a child do a jigsaw. The good parent does not just complete the jigsaw for their child. This would be a humiliating disruption of the infant's curiosity and play, possibly disabling them for life if routinely repeated. Instead, the grown-up presents a piece of the jigsaw for the child's contemplation, perhaps with a hint or suggestion as to how it might fit in. Or if a piece has been forced into the wrong place, the mistake is gently drawn attention to in such a way that the child can learn from the error.

Similarly, according to Plato, Socrates was very good at this enabling didactic role. In the literature, it is referred to as Socratic irony, the word 'irony' meaning that like any good teacher, Socrates suspended what he thought he knew about a particular issue, and so was free to get alongside others, help them, and move forward himself with them too. He confessed that by assisting others he always learnt something new. For example, in the *Lysis* – having sympathised with the bind the love-struck Hippothales is in – Socrates goes on to talk to the young man Lysis about friendship. How does this crucial, invaluable love work, they ask?

At first, Lysis reflects that his close friendships seem to be based upon similarities. Like with like together strike. Birds of a feather flock together. But wouldn't those relationships become boring, Socrates wonders, and friendship isn't like that. Oh yes, Lysis continues. Perhaps then, it's actually our differences that fire our friendships. The dry desert longs for the wet rain. That sounds like a richer idea, Socrates replies, only something must draw friends together. We can't be completely different. But how can we share our experience and feel connected without denying each his or her own? The conversation develops as the relationships they know in their lives are explored, not to reach final answers but to enlarge the sense of them.

A closure – arriving at a definite understanding of friendship – would kill the possibility of forming actual friends. It would be like the self-help advice proffered these days in which an expert tells you how many friends you need, and then tells you how to go out and get them. Who wants to be friends with someone who knows all about friendship, or who treats you as a service provider in their self-referential life? Rather, Plato's advice – modeled in the dialogue – is rather like the aphorism of Ralph Waldo Emerson: 'The only way to have a friend is to be one.' By chewing over his actual friendships, particularly in their uncomfortable or difficult moments, the midwife Socrates helps Lysis to become a better friend by being wiser and so more capable of friendship.

To put it another way, Plato strove to ensure that his readers – meaning us – would not lift philosophy directly from the page, like the fundamentalist does a text from their sacred book, but would engage with the dialogue so as to cultivate wisdom in their own life. John Stuart Mill described the process well in his pamphlet, *On Liberty*. Plato produced brilliant discussions of the great questions of philosophy and life, Mill writes, 'to the purpose of convincing anyone who had merely adopted the commonplaces of received opinion that he did not understand the subject.' Get to that place, and life can offer you more.

The principle extends to Plato's political writings as well as those focused on more spiritual or personal subjects like love. It's worth pausing here, because the dialogue of Plato that is most commonly read today is one of the political ones, the *Republic*. And because the reflexive quality of Plato's method is missed when it is read, I think it is routinely misunderstood.

The mistake is to treat it as a manifesto and, to the liberal mind, a deeply unpleasant one at that. This view was spread by one of the twentieth century's great champions of freedom, the philosopher Karl Popper. A central plank of Popper's defence of freedom was a fierce attack on what he called 'utopian social engineering'. And in his 1945 best-seller, *The Open Society*, he cast Plato as villain-in-chief, the originator of a form of totalitarian politics that in our times came to threaten the whole world. In short, Plato's *Republic* shows him up as an armchair Stalin, responsible for nurturing the dream of all subsequent dictators, that they could design an ideal state that would never decay.

Never mind that when Popper wrote *The Open Society* he did not have to hand a decent translation of the *Republic*, as he admits in his autobiography, *Unended Quest*. Or that 'what I read was determined largely by what books I could get in New Zealand', which was limited because of the war. Subsequent generations of English-speaking philosophers have picked up the main drift and tended to follow Popper's line. Plato is taken as having started a lust for central planning that is a dangerous mistake. It could be said to be indirectly responsible for the deaths of millions.

But the tragedy is that, properly understood, the *Republic* is designed precisely to guard against social engineering. It relentlessly exposes the folly of human ignorance that believes it can design a society and manipulate life. Plato has one of his characters in the *Republic* explicitly comment that such a city-state as they have been describing will never, in actuality, be found. It is a utopia, to use Thomas More's word, meaning literally a 'no-place'. It is another manifestation of Socratic irony.

In fact, it is only relatively recently that the *Republic* has been interpreted this way, and that reading Plato has become so distorted. It seems that the *Republic* was adopted by the Victorian public school system as an ur-text for the young men who were being trained to govern the British empire. They had the Bible to shape their souls and the *Republic* to hone their leadership. Before then, the *Republic* had been treated as an exercise in fantasy politics, an attempt to expose what is at stake in political philosophy, rather than an attempt to write a manifesto upon which Plato might stand for election to office. In that former sense, it has been very successful. It put justice, education and the good firmly on the political agenda. Plato was writing an extended thought experiment out of which to develop resources to critique the politics of the real world you know. In the utopia, society is structure so that its leaders can manifest the virtues. It is imagined as being ruled by guardians – men and women who as individuals already know what's good and so are in a position to nurture the good across the rest of society. These mythical philosopher-kings and philosopher-queens lead a dedicated existence so as to vouchsafe the goodness of their rule. They have no private family life. They have no private property. Private possessions lead to vested interests, division and strife. Any actual politics must remember that.

The guardians are the first of three classes narrated in the *Republic*. Beneath them comes the soldier class, who would share in the educative ideals of the guardians. And third, comes the class of economically active individuals. They make up the bulk of society and form the professionals, the artisans and the property-holders. This strict division of labour is designed to ensure that the lofty task of ruling the city-state does not become embroiled in the humdrum business of the marketplace, those activities which generate wealth, and with that run the risks of corruption. Again, it's another useful marker – difficult to put into practice, in fact always likely to fail, but essential to hold onto as an ethical principle. Fifth century BC Athens. Twenty-first century late capitalism. Spot the difference. That's what the *Republic* asks us to do.

At this point, it's worth saying something about another group of philosophers who also understood the spirit of Socrates but interpreted his calling to understand ignorance in a different way from Plato. They were the Sceptics, which means searchers, and could be said to have argued that uncertainty was best if simply embraced. Forget trying to become wisely involved in politics. It is hubris to believe that possible. Forget trying to cultivate the force called love. It is untamable and wild. Instead, suspend everything you think you know and, as a by-product, an inner tranquility will be the result.

The approach was promoted by a philosopher called Pyrrho, and is sometimes known as Pyrrhonism. (For the sake of clarity, Pyrrho's scepticism needs to be distinguished from another form of ancient scepticism, now called 'Academic Scepticism'. That sprang from a reform of Plato's Academy in the third century BC, holding that whilst there might be truth, no one position can capture that truth fully. So they made Socratic questioning a way of life, rather than suspending belief like the Pyrrhonists.) Pyrrho was born a few decades after the death of Socrates, and travelled to the East with the armies of Alexander the Great. There he met the Indian gymnosophists and was profoundly challenged by their rejection of the material world and devotion to thought and contemplation. He returned to Athens, and seems to have developed a Socratic version of their unattached indifference. The Sceptic took life at face value. He or she did not speculate about physical causes, metaphysical meanings, or epistemological foundations.

We can only know how things appear. We cannot know whether our senses speak truthfully or lie. And that is enough to live.

It's a strikingly different approach to Plato. He agreed that we are surrounded by ignorance but argued that reason might help us to penetrate our unknowns. Philosophy for him is about discernment, not disinterest. The lover of wisdom can come close to what he or she seeks, he averred, though it ultimately eludes them. The Sceptics rejected even that asymptotic approach.

They have found followers throughout history, particularly in the Renaissance. Michel de Montaigne read about Pyrrhonism and invented the essay, a form of writing that tries or essays its subject matter. I think of Sigmund Freud as a kind of Sceptic too, he developing the psychoanalytic technique of releasing and then questioning what his patient's felt to be true about their lives, though was causing them great problems. Many artists might be practicing Sceptics too, if they feel their work comes from a place of not-knowing, but exploring indirectly. Suspend what you think you know, enter the place of unknowing, and surprising novelty may result.

Plato's didactic intentions, his ironic, educative stance, did not have the same aim as the Sceptics. For him, philosophy was full of doubts, but also held the possibility of revelation. So, to come back to Plato, can we say anything about what he himself came to believe and perceive? I think we can, indirectly.

His personal formation with Socrates, and then alongside others in the Academy – their ethical and spiritual transformation facilitated by the intellectual and rational task – must have produced some fairly steady conclusions. In fact, there is one piece of prose writing that survives and is almost certainly authentically by him, the so-called *Seventh Letter* (the others have been discredited). In that, he describes how this philosophical life ignites a flame in the soul. With that light, it is possible to see more deeply. The inner kindling is essential, he explains. Describing his philosophy as a set of dry doctrines – Plato believed x, y, z – will inevitably miss the point. What you can say about the experience is always going to be a bit clumsy, rather second best. Creedal summaries of it will sound as arbitrary and strange as the ancient Greek's belief in a god called Zeus sitting on Mount Olympus does to us. But that is not to say that nothing can be said. If we keep one eye firmly on the way, the other may detect some of the epistemological results and struggle to give them articulation. The process, alongside some of the results, is described in one of Plato's best known myths, that of the cave, also from the *Republic*.

The story depicts most human beings as living as if imprisoned at the back of a cave. They are pinned down, though unknowingly, so that all they can see are the shadows dancing on the back wall. That's all they have ever known, and so they take the shadows to be real.

However, prisoners are sometimes freed. They struggle, pained, and manage to look around. Behind them, they see a fire, and in front of the fire, puppets. Immediately, shockingly, they realise that what they had thought was real is a delusion. It sets them on a quest.

They must struggle much more. In fact, the reluctance and fear of the freed prisoner is emphasized throughout the allegory. It's hard to shift perspective, not to see life through the assumptions you have adopted as true. It's easier to insist the world is red than to admit you are wearing red-tinted spectacles. And the new colours are, at first, just as much disorientating glare. But the lucky prisoners persist and are helped, and they next notice something else, utterly unexpected. They see a steady source of even radiance. Drawn by its beauty, in the way that only beauty can carry us towards what's unknown but new, they then find themselves on the brink of another experience that is simultaneously appealing and bewildering. The radiance is an opening. The cave has a mouth. And outside lies a larger world, a much, much larger world. It is lit by a source so dazzling that it blinds to stare at directly. And yet, this sunlight fills everything – warms everything, colours everything, bathes everything with life.

It is a spiritual revelation, the implication being that if we allow Plato's methods, and Socrates' spirit, to form us, we will embark upon a journey that transforms everything by exposing us to the transcendent implicit in everyday life. We will develop the eyes to see it.

That is the result. In various places, Plato attempts to describe it using a metaphor now known as the Forms. The idea is that when you see something you perceive to be good or beautiful or true – perhaps a good person, a beautiful scene, a true insight – it resonates so powerfully with us because it is also a reflection of that which is good, beautiful and true in the utmost. Hence the Form of Good, Beauty and Truth is what we human beings are most deeply drawn to, though we resist the pull too because it can simultaneously feel like too much.

In a way, the notion of Forms is Plato's attempt to reconcile Heraclitus' sense that the world is in a state of flux with Parmenides' reasoning that all is one. At one level, change and chaos is what we see. At another, a unified harmony can be glimpsed tangentially. Plato himself does not call this awesome confluence of perfection divine, though subsequent readers have resorted to the word 'God'. That can be a helpful thought for some. Another follower of Plato, Plotinus, who founded the tradition now known as Neoplatonism, talked of 'The One'. 'The chief difficulty is this,' he said according to the *Enneads*, a record of his life. 'Awareness of The One comes to us neither by knowing nor by the pure thought that discovers the other intelligible things, but by a presence ... That is why Plato says of The

One, "It can neither be spoken of nor written about." If nevertheless we speak of it and write about it, we do so only to give direction, to urge towards that vision beyond discourse, to point out the road to one desirous of seeing ...'

The former prisoners, now enlightened, see it. They want to rush back to their fellows, still held at the back of the cave, and tell them: there is more to life than you can ever imagine. But then things turn bad. The remaining prisoners do not want to be told that they are mistaken. They like their bonds, feel secure in the shadows. That's rubbish, they say to those who have returned from above. Where's the evidence? Where's the reasoning that will persuade me you are right?

But you can only know if you go on the journey, the enlightened ones reply. It's worth remembering that the word theory in Plato's time, *theoria*, did not mean an abstract formulation that could be tested for its veracity, like Newton's second law of motion. Rather, it was a trip you undertook, the experience itself being the agent of change, of expansion, of discovery. The *theoria* with which Plato's first readers would have been most familiar was that of the Eleusinian mysteries, the initiation ceremonies involving fasting and journeying and consuming a sacred drink that imparted such a dramatic experience of life and death that a transformed awareness of them was born. The implication is that Plato felt that Socrates had introduced a new set of mysteries. They myth of the cave dramatises what it was like to follow him, to be exposed to his charisma and presence. And indeed, in the story, the returning initiates come to a sticky end, as Socrates had done. They are killed by the prisoners who prefer to remain in the dark.

It sounds very religious and I'd say that is right. 'Socrates and Plato were shocked by the sophists because they had no religious aims,' observed the twentieth century philosopher, Bertrand Russell, who was an agnostic himself. For those who feel ambivalent about the r-word, it's worth remembering that winning any kind of new knowledge above the humdrum requires embarking on a process that is, at the very least, a kind of initiation – enabling sight of what could not have been seen before. To become a physicist or mathematician, biologist or naturalist, takes a long training and apprenticeship. It is a question of temperament and character as much as ability and learning. Also, from the outside, the truths divined by these disciplines can appear as esoteric as any spiritual insight. The difference is that, these days, we trust scientists more than priests because we trust the material more than the spiritual.

Plato was also very aware that those who claim to be enlightened can readily be misled. In the *Symposium*, he implies that those who feel they have detected what is truly beautiful, who claim to have seen the light, should be wary lest they simply be spiritually drunk. A trip on LSD would not have been regarded as trustworthy by him, because the off-your-face element would mean the individual could not practice discernment. The slow, purgative task of collective contemplation and individual meditation seems to have been his preferred route, his followers being remembered for exercising daily periods of silence.

And finally, Plato did not want his followers to accept on trust. It is a striking fact that he never says anything in his own voice in his dialogues. He only appears three times, and then in the background, in passing. He is like Shakespeare, disappearing in his own work. The upshot is that asking what Plato really thought is a bit like asking whether Shakespeare was a Protestant or Catholic. It'll never finally be settled in an objective sense. The individual can only know because they know in themselves. Go to the play and then you get Shakespeare. So too, 'Platonism' is not a set of doctrines that can be accepted or dismissed by its coherence and consistency. It is a training, an illumination, a path.

4.

Aristotle on happiness and plots

I have been more than hinting that Plato is not much in favour amongst professional philosophers these days. Religious experience and spiritual discernment is not really their milieu, and to be fair, there is a lot more to Plato and following Socrates than soulful insight. We'll come to some of that now, in thinking about Aristotle, Plato's greatest pupil, and how he took on Plato's lead particularly in his great interest in anything and everyday in the natural world, and also the question of how to live well in it. (His followers became known as the Peripatetics, those who walk around, which might mean that they thought best when perambulating or, metaphorically, that the school ranged widely over many subjects. Or both.)

You may know the famous fresco of Raphael in the Vatican, entitled The School of Athens. Centre stage stand Plato and Aristotle, the first perched on his toes, his finger pointing to heaven; the second palm faced down, his feet firmly on the ground. It highlights presumed differences between the two, though in truth, these two followers of Socrates have much more in common than distinguishes them, if only because Plato, having sat at the feet of Socrates for a couple of decades, then had Aristotle sit at his feet for a couple more until 347 BC: Aristotle was a member of the Academy until Plato died, only then setting up his own school, the Lyceum – which he may have done having expected to be elected the Academy's second head, a honour that passed to another, Speusippus, Plato's nephew.

For example, in his *Nicomachean Ethics*, a set of remembered lectures on how to cultivate happiness and flourish, Aristotle concludes, 'we must not follow those who advise us, being men, to think of human things, and, being mortal, of mortal things, but must, so far as we can, make ourselves immortal, and strain every nerve to live in accordance with the best thing in us.' A life in touch with the divine, being pleasurable and best, is the richest. Plato would have concurred. In the medieval period, too, when Islamic civilisation preserved and developed ancient Greek culture whilst Europe reeled after the collapse of the Roman empire, Aristotle was known simply as 'the philosopher'. In those theological times, he was regarded as eminent.

And yet, there is something in Aristotle that is more earthy, and so more to modern tastes. For one thing, the texts that survive are not literary, like Plato's, but are lectures, field notes, dissertations. Though not such a good read, they fit more readily with our philosophical preferences and styles. He did write dialogues, apparently with a brilliance to match his predecessor, it is just that they have not survived the intervening centuries. One of history's great losses. I think of him having a different temperament to Plato. He seems to have been the kind of person who trusted his senses, gaining his information about the world by observing and probing and collecting. Plato was different in that he naturally turned to his powerful intuitive capacities. Perhaps that was the fundamental difference between them.

Aristotle was well served in his more empirical method because one of his own pupils was Alexander the Great. He had been called to teach the budding conqueror when Alexander was a young man because Aristotle's father had been a physician in the Macedonian court. So when Alexander went on to create a massive empire, seventy to eighty years after the death of Socrates, he remembered his old tutor. Alexander had samples of flora and fauna, as well as case studies of political constitutions and even types of friendship, sent back from Asia Minor and Egypt, from Persia and the Hindu Kush, to Aristotle's various bases – sometimes in Athens, sometimes in other cities around the eastern Mediterranean. (Aristotle had to flee Athens for his life on at least two occasions. He upset quite as many people as Socrates.)

In fact, there's a neat piece of archeology that captures the ups and downs of Aristotle's public reception. A plaque commemorating some work he did on the history of the Pythian games was discovered down a well at Delphi. The plaque thanked him and one of his nephews for their sterling public service. Only, the reason the honour survives is because it must have subsequently been hurled down the well. As Heraclitus' might note: nothing stands still, not least a reputation.

His reputation today has shifted again since the high days of the medieval period when he was 'the philosopher'. These days, much of his work on the natural world has been superseded by the assumptions and methods of modern science. But let's gain more of a sense of his philosophy with an area of research that he made his own when he was alive, and to which modern philosophers still turn, namely virtue ethics.

In the ancient world, in fact right up to the eighteenth century, this was the main of doing ethics. It emphasizes how people perform good acts, and generally flourish in life, because of the character and habits they embody in their person. An analogy Aristotle employs is that of an archer. A good bowman is the person who has put in the hours of practice and training, as well as put up with the countless mistakes and mishits. Only now can they hit the target reliably and accurately. They have developed a skill, one that enables them to have a good chance of landing a bullseye whether the weather is still or blustery, whether the competition is friendly or pressured.

Similarly in ethics. The good warrior, Aristotle continues with another example, exhibits the virtue of courage. That means they are the person who knows in the heat of battle how to behave neither in a foolhardy manner, plunging unthinkingly into the midst of the fighting, nor in a timid manner, edging cowardly in the opposite direction. They will, spontaneously, assess what's at stake and what part they can perform, and courageously play their part to the full. Incidentally, this analysis of the virtues as the midpoint between two extremes – courage being neither foolhardiness nor cowardliness – is known as Aristotle's doctrine of the mean.

It's a question of one's disposition too, virtuous behaviour being supported by appropriate feelings. I particularly like the way in which the medieval philosopher, Thomas Aquinas, took Aristotle's method and applied it to the Christian virtue of hope. There are two related aspects to hope, Aquinas noted, one a habit of mind, the other a feeling. The habit of mind is the commitment the hopeful person makes to that which they hope for. It brings focus and confidence. But it must be supported by the feeling that though what we hope for may be difficult to achieve, it will be worth the effort. This passion helps the individual to rise to the challenge, and overcome fear or despair.

What this adds up to is that the virtuous life requires an education not only of the body and mind but of the heart too. This then enables someone in knowing how to hold fast to what they regard as good, though with a flexibility that also enables them to respond to whatever life throws at them – the chance events that always threaten to undo us. The good friend, in another scenario Aristotle discusses, understands that mostly he should be open and honest with others, though sometimes he might hold back – not because he is being dishonest, but because he realises that honesty requires him to admit that on this occasion he is not quite sure what he thinks, and so is not quite sure what to say for the best.

In Aristotle's time, virtue was its own reward. Today, though, two different ethical systems have risen to the fore. One is utilitarian ethics, in which an action is deemed good if it increases people's pleasure and decreases pain. This approach does not advocate character training. Instead, it judges according to what might bring the greatest happiness to the greatest number. It's a natural assumption to make, and a pragmatic one in an otherwise plural world. After all, everyone wants to be happy, many presume, regardless of race or creed, of socio-economic position or political persuasion. The risk, though, is that such calculations end up having little to do with ethics, and individuals increasingly behave according to what they think they can get away with. So long as it hurts no-one, or not too many, it is alright. Bankers become more wealthy. Arms dealers increase their trade. Human relationships are corrupted in a thousand petty ways.

Second is deontological ethics, coming from the Greek *deon*, or 'duty'. This approach argues that an ethical act is one that is done from a sense of obligation. It is not the consequences of an act that count, therefore, but the motivations that lie behind it. Pleasure, for example, cannot be a measure of ethical worth because some people take pleasure in despicable things, such as the pain of others. Reality TV makes an industry out of it. But the trouble with deontological ethics is that our motivations are rarely pure. Have you ever performed a wholly altruistic act? Virtue ethics seems to have a more realistic grip on human nature, positively encouraging people to make mistakes and struggle with compromise because they then learn, then their character develops. For such reasons, philosophers these days are returning to virtue ethics, and with it the insights of Aristotle.

But still, it leaves hanging the question of why we might want to put in all the effort to become more virtuous, to have the practical intelligence to know how to behave skillfully? The answer, in a word, is happiness – though Aristotle's term, *eudaimonia*, is richer than that modern translation implies. *Eudaimonia* literally means good-godedness. It does not much imply feeling good or even contented, as if life should contain more pleasure than pain. The life of the warrior, or that of a parent, might well hold the prospect of lots of trouble and suffering. Aristotle doesn't deny that pleasure is welcome when it comes, but it does come and go, and so orientating your life around it is inevitably limiting. Also, there are deeper pleasures felt not so much at the level of emotion as of the soul. They, though it might seem hard to admit, often co-exist with kinds of pain. 'In every painting a whole is mysteriously enclosed, a whole life of tortures, doubts, of hours of enthusiasm and inspiration,' wrote the artist Wassily Kandinsky. But artists with their doubts, alongside many other forms of life and the associated tortures, may all flourish, reach their potential, taste the experience of feeling fully human.

Another intriguing element in Aristotle's conception of how to live well is that it embraced the arts, and in particular that of the poet and playwright. He became fascinated with the impact that plots have upon us. If he was living today, I think he would be as interested in funding the arts for civic education, as much as in schools. He would be as worried about the stories adults tell themselves each day in newspapers and magazines, as much as the narratives inherent in the computer games that so engage our kids.

He realised that to expose yourself to a drama, be it fictional or fact, is to be shaped by it. It gets under your skin, it quickens or chills your heart. We talk of compassion fatigue, after too many tales of poverty. Alternatively, the story of an athlete's struggle and Olympic success might inspire the next generation.

He thought that plots work, first, because human beings are

mimetic creatures. We love to learn about others' stories, not only because in them we see reflected our own, but because we spontaneously copy or define ourselves against others. It probably starts very young, as imitation fills our early life. A baby jiggles up and down. Mummy claps her hands, matching the rhythm and pattern. Copying creates a sense of connection and intimacy, and so it is closely aligned to happiness for the rest of our lives.

Then, dramas also help us to express our emotions, to be alleviated of the burden of them, and to refine them. He called this catharsis. He was particularly struck by the place of tragedy in ancient Athenian society, the great plays of Aeschylus and Sophocles. They portray the terrible things that can happen to people as a result of war, madness, or calamity. Watching Sophocles' *Oedipus Rex*, Aristotle's idea of a masterpiece, and you feel rung out by the end. The man is fated from birth to kill his father and have children by his mother, and you feel the horror coming, until at the last he takes out his eyes. Why do we watch such tales? Because, in them, we virtually experience some of our own fears, without undergoing the actual consequences. This is beneficial because it may save us from ourselves, or at least prepare us for life's inevitable tragedies. 'A tragedy is a representation of a grand, complete, and significant action ... with episodes arousing pity and fear so as to achieve purification [catharsis] of these emotions,' Aristotle explains in his slightly dry prose.

There's a third element that a really good story builds in. He calls it reversal and recognition. These are the moments when the plot falls into place, when all the pieces that seem scattered suddenly make sense, though they can do so with a judder of horror. This is precisely what happens to Oedipus. He hears of the death of Polybus by natural causes and, thinking he's his father, welcomes the news. The oracle is proven wrong. He is not a parricide. Only, next he prompts the messenger to tell more of the story. More details emerge, in particular that the dead Polybus was an adoptive parent. The detail that seemed good turns bad.

This is an education because life is like that. Human beings are the in between creatures, the ones who never know the full truth. Like Plato and Socrates before him, Aristotle feels that no education is complete without the effort to increase self-awareness of our many ignorances. Stories are another powerful way to do so.

5.

Epicureans and the pursuit of pleasure

You'll remember Parmenides, the presocratic who insisted that reason tells us there is no such thing as change because something cannot come from nothing. Aristotle disagreed with him. The solution, the peripatetic suggested, is to think not in terms of nothing, which like Parmenides he also felt was an empty concept, but instead in terms of potential. Life is full of potential – of possibilities – Aristotle felt. In fact, life could be defined as a kind of energy and activity that brings change about, and change is what happens when what is potential becomes actual, when life's potency makes itself manifest. It's part of the dynamic, animated vision of the natural world that Aristotle envisaged.

So, a man may or may not become a father, though if he does he certainly changes, or we'd hope so. The mud may or may not produce oysters (Aristotle believed that some creatures self-generate from putrefying earth), but if it does there is now an oyster bed that was only potentially there before. All acorns have the potential to grow into an oak, but it is the one that actually does which offers you rest in its shade. More subtly, Aristotle also thought that creatures, not least human beings, can often be said not to live up to their potential when they fall short, in some way. 'Sometimes we say that those who can walk or speak cannot walk or speak, because they do it not as well as they intended,' he observes. It is part of the loss inherent in life that all sorts of capabilities and possibilities remain undeveloped. Most seeds don't germinate, they rot. The young of many animals do not make it adulthood, but die. Many human lives are ruined by the intervention of tragedy.

Other ways of resolving the paradoxes of change, and the relationship between something and nothing, were pursued too. And here we come to a new figure, because another important development, that takes our story onto different terrain, is associated with our next philosopher, Epicurus, and his followers, the Epicureans.

They were the thorough-going materialists of the ancient world, so offer a distinctly contrasting worldview from Socrates, Plato, and Aristotle. By materialism they meant not only that the world is made of matter but that this matter interacts in mechanistic ways. (The Stoics, to whom we come shortly, were also materialists of sorts, though their materialism was more organic and teleological, including divine forces in nature.) How so? Well, the Epicureans were atomists. They held that there is a basic unit of matter that is indivisible and indestructible – 'atom' in ancient Greek just meaning indivisible. These atoms move in a void, mostly in straight lines, but sometimes swerving when they collide and coalesce, like billiard balls. Though we have no perception of this movement, because it happens on tiny scales, it nonetheless underpins all the gross features of the world that we observe at the macro level.

What the inference that there are atoms has to do with something and nothing can be explained via a thought experiment. Imagine you are holding a sheet of paper. You tear it in half. Then you tear one half into half again. And again, and again, and again. You keep going. The Epicurean would argue that you couldn't keep going on *ad infinitum*, even in theory, because that would mean you would finally be left with nothing in your hand. And before you had something, a piece of paper. Hence, because something cannot become nothing, in the same way that nothing cannot produce something, there must be a point at which the torn paper will become as small as an atom, and so become untearable anymore.

There were other reasons you might believe in atoms though you can't see them. They explain why the cosmos constantly changes and yet also constantly renews itself. It's just atoms in a continual dance of disintegration and reorganization. The beauty of this notion struck some powerfully, not least the Roman poet Lucretius. His work, *On the Nature of Things*, is one of the key and most compelling sources of Epicurean thought. Here's what he has to say about this distinctive feature of the Epicurean universe (in the translation by W. E. Leonard):

> For since they wander through the void inane,
> All the primordial germs of things must needs
> Be borne along, either by weight their own,
> Or haply by another's blow without.
> For, when, in their incessancy so oft
> They meet and clash, it comes to pass again
> They leap asunder, face to face: not strange—
> Being most hard, and solid in their weights,
> And naught opposing motion, from behind.
> And that more clearly thou perceive how all
> These mites of matter are darted round about,
> Recall to mind how nowhere in the sum
> Of All exists a bottom,—nowhere is
> A realm of rest for primal bodies; since
> (As amply shown and proved by reason sure)
> Space has no bound nor measure, and extends
> Unmetered forth in all directions round.

You notice how Lucretius weaves in other aspects of Epicurean cosmology too, such as the infinity of space. This means that there is no 'fine tuning' in the universe to produce us. It is a deterministic place. We just happen to live where the atoms have randomly come together to form us, as of course we must.

Atomic theory is another way of responding to Socrates' sense that the human condition is one of ignorance and doubt. The random motion and mechanistic interactions of the atoms, moving by chance not guided by fate, is experienced by us as a life of uncertainty because there is no telling what constellation or pattern may form next. Atoms behave 'haply', by accident. So does life.

That said, Epicurus did not see himself as a follower of Socrates. The Epicureans strove to distinguish themselves from the Athenian sage and his disciples, partly out of loyalty to Epicurus' claim to have been entirely self-taught, a reflection of his conviction that philosophy must be rooted in one's own observation of the world not in an inherited tradition; and partly, contrariwise, out of an extraordinary devotion the Epicureans showed to Epicurus himself. He was born around 60 years after the death of Socrates, growing up on the island of Samos, and coming to Athens around 320 BC, and must have been remarkably charismatic. Lucretius describes him as a saviour of humankind, as a father, and a god – the only word that can capture his qualities and the fact that he brought a heaven-like life of tranquility and bliss to earth. For centuries, Epicurus' birthday was kept like a saint's day.

He set up a philosophical school called the Garden. It was outside the city walls because, Epicurus said, the first thing a philosopher needs is to be free of distractions. The city is, therefore, the worse place to try to reconstruct your life. It is impossible to think amidst its hubbub for yourself. In the Garden, they not only lived simply but did more practical things, like tend crops for food. There is a strong strand of what you might call collective individualism in Epicureanism, a self-sufficiency that individuals pursue together. It is easy to imagine the satisfaction of such a life from our own period of history, and its manic city-life. Little wonder, too, that Karl Marx wrote his PhD on Epicureanism. He felt that human beings cease to feel alienated from the world only when they are materially engaged with the world.

The emphasis on natural asceticism – living simply – may strike you as anomalous, given that Epicurus' name today is associated with almost the opposite way of life. An epicure, now, is synonymous with a foodie or gourmand. In fact, and as a general principle, it is worth remembering that several of the names of the ancient philosophical schools and their founders have become skewed across the centuries. If the Epicureans were actually ascetics, the Stoics did not believe in the stiff upper lip, the Cynics were not cynical, and the Sceptics did not go around debunking other people's beliefs. It's already been said that the Sceptics derive their name from searcher. The origins of the Stoic and Cynic names await us. The Epicureans were named after Epicurus, of course, and they were misunderstood right from the start – not as proponents of less is more, but the opposite philosophy, that more is more. The difficulty seems to have been that Epicurus invited women and slaves to join him in the Garden. Like Socrates and Plato, he felt that all human beings could be educated in philosophical ways. But it was an unboundaried welcome that must have aroused great suspicion in a culture where woman were generally not seen alone in public and slaves were, well, owned. So what else would a man want with women and slaves, in an eccentric, secret little commune away from the city, if not indulgent and nefarious activities?

In truth, Epicurus' motto might have been live simply. If physics is, at base, simple – atoms moving in a void – then life is, at base, simple too, he proposed. It's just a question of pleasure. That's what human beings want. The question is how to cultivate a way of life that is pleasurable without inadvertently simultaneously nurturing the complex and disastrous cravings, habits and addictions to pleasure that so easily distort a life?

His answer was a kind of therapy. His philosophical way of life was a steady, thorough remedy for excess. It was summed up by another, later follower, Philodemus of Gadara, who became an inhabitant of Herculaneum in the first century BC. Many of his works were found in a library preserved by the eruption of Vesuvius, and include what he called the *tetrapharmakos*, or four-fold cure. Philodemus presented Epicurus' philosophy as a medicine promoting the particular pleasure known as *ataraxia* – tranquility or peaceableness. It has four active ingredients.

- First, don't fear the gods. They are not out to get you. When stuff happens it is just chance. Moreover, why should gods care much for us? They live in bliss already and so are hardly likely to become embroiled in the pains of human affairs.

- Second, don't fear death. It is only the dissolution of that agglomeration of atoms you call 'me'. In the same way that there was nothing conscious of you before your life, so there will be nothing of you afterwards. Nothing to fear.

- Third, what is good is easy to get. This is the simple pleasures message. Epicurus had argued that what we need to live well is usually pretty easily secured. Water. Food. Shelter. Friends. He once said he could be as happy as Zeus feasting on Mount Olympus if all he had was a glass of water and a barley cake.

- Fourth, what is dreadful is easy to endure. This is perhaps the most tricky of the ingredients to swallow, though remember that Epicurus offered a training to help you reach this goal. You weren't expected to realise it overnight. What he seems to have meant is that most of human suffering arises from the anticipation of pain, rather than from the pain itself which, when it comes, is often surprisingly more easy to bear than we might anticipate. Epicurus demonstrated as much himself. One of the texts in his own hand that survives to our day is a letter written on the last day of his life. He had a urinary complaint, probably kidney stones, and was in terrible pain – except, he confessed, the remembrance of the joys of friendship were so alive in his mind that they kept the pain and the proximity of death in check. He died a happy man.

It's possible to deepen this Epicurean 'hedonism', which is important to do, I think, because it can come across as an abnegation of life, a reduction of what matters to a creed that implies little matters. After all, surely death is to be feared, if not your own then the death of those whom you love? Or are good things always simple and easy to get? Take friendship. It's free, yes. But the intimacy of soul mates is often hard won, and at the very least, takes time.

The Epicureans distinguished between different types of pleasure, distinctions that are useful in the cultivation of the tranquil life. For example, bodily pleasures are different from mental pleasures. Hence, on his deathbed, Epicurus did not enjoy many bodily pleasures, not least because bodily pleasures and pains tend to be generated by what's happening here and now. But he had access to mental pleasures too, a type of experience that extends over time and space because it is carried inside: Epicurus remembers his friendship. In general, Epicureans felt that mental pleasures are more powerful than bodily pains, a key hierarchy if the inevitable discomforts of life are to be born calmly. One set of exercises they performed together were visualisations, nurturing the capacity to vividly recall pleasurable memories at will.

Pleasures could also be divided between the kinetic and the katastematic or static. The former kinetic, from the word for motion, are pleasures that are satisfied by doing something. Life is full of them. Drinking a glass of water to satisfy a thirst. Securing the land for your philosophical garden to lead the Epicurean way of life. They are necessary but not really sufficient for reaching *ataraxia*. That is secured by static pleasures. They depend more on being than doing, on an inner stillness rather than an outer activity. In this sense, Epicureanism has a spiritual dimension too. It has an inward turn that proved powerful in the Hellenistic world in which Epicureanism first flourished. After the conquests of Alexander, the city-states known by Socrates and loved by Aristotle were sucked into the machinery of empire and lost their autonomy, so it became risky to rely on the political community to support your quest for the good life. But if you developed an inner flourishing, that gave you resilience against the turbulence of external events.

The shift proved highly influential in the ancient world as the Macedonian empire was replaced by the Roman, and Epicureanism became second only to Stoicism, another 'inner' philosophy, in terms of its popularity. It only fell behind when Christianity established itself. Communities of Epicureans were known across the Mediterranean region, though alongside the dedicated followers of Epicurus were many more who selected bits of his advice to enhance their lives. They inscribed his sayings on walls and etched prompts on rings and bracelets, like mantras that might slowly change you inside. The links Epicurus developed between the materialist physics of atoms, the simple pleasures of his ethics, and the humanistic goals of his philosophy, may resonate with you too.

6.

Going with the flow. The Stoics and Cynics

Time for another philosophy. Time for another story.

Life did not appear to be going well for Zeno of Citium. Born just after Epicurus, almost 70 years after the death of Socrates and 15 years since the death of Plato, he seemed condemned to life as a merchant. His father traded in the reddish-purple semi-precious stone, porphyry. The son felt he had to maintain the family business, though he strained to leave Citium, on the island of Cyprus, precisely because his father's trading expeditions around the Mediterranean brought philosophy into their home. The patriarch of the family had an interest in philosophy and on his trips would often buy manuscripts of Plato's dialogues. The young Zeno devoured them and longed to get to Athens. The home of Socrates felt very distant.

Things got worse. Zeno was now undertaking expeditions himself. The Mediterranean was the ancient European world's highway, but it was a dangerous one, populated by natural and human threats: storms and pirates. One day, Zeno was caught in a storm. His ship was wrecked. To a life of frustration was added disaster.

Only, he managed to save himself and swimming ashore realised that his ship had gone down off coast from Piraeus. The port of Athens.

He followed the walls that led into the city, and found his way into a bookshop. The story goes that he picked up a collection of memoirs by Xenophon, a soldier who had known Socrates. The buzz of reading of the man, from a first hand witness, in the city of his birth was overwhelming. When a wild-looking character passed by the shop door, and the bookseller told him that was a follower of Socrates, Zeno immediately took after him.

He was called Crates. 'I want to follow Socrates,' Zeno said. 'Here. Hold this bowl of lentil stew,' Crates replied. An unexpected instruction, but Zeno obliged.

After an hour, he became embarrassed. After another, annoyed. He tried to hide the bowl, juggling it this way and that. Crates noticed. With a single swipe, he smashed the pottery. The mess dribbled down Zeno's tunic.

Humiliated now, any residual enthusiasm was shattered in new waves of frustration. 'What's wrong,' Crates retorted coolly. 'Nothing terrible has happened' – for he was a Cynic, a pun on the Greek for dogs because these philosophers lived like them, it was said. They interpreted Socrates' uncertainty to imply that social mores and conventions trap us. How we eat, the way we dress, where we live, who we marry. The myriad of unwritten rules hold us hostage in rigid customs that are actually as ill-founded as any intellectual claims, be they from sophists, politicians or poets. Be freed from them, the Cynics taught. They did so by showing how they were free of them themselves. Lentils dripping down your front was a mild humiliation compared to some of the ordeals a Cynic might endure.

For Zeno, it was too much. But the story does not end there. He preserved a sense of the importance of ascetics from Crates, though in the days and weeks that followed his arrival in Athens decided that not all conventions are bad. Most simply don't matter that much.

A less extreme philosophy of life began to emerge. Zeno took to sitting in the marketplace in the shade of one of the painted colonnades or *stoa*. Soon, he attracted followers. Stoicism was born, the philosophical school that turned into the most successful of them all in the Greco-Roman world. Around 350 years later, the Stoic called Seneca was summoned to tutor the emperor. (Unfortunately for him, that emperor was Nero.) Another century on, and a Stoic became emperor, Marcus Aurelius. Zeno had born frustration, disaster and humiliation with just enough patience. His life turned out alright.

This 'biography' of Zeno is impossible to verify. It's told by Diogenes Laertius, a third century CE collector of myths and fables, teachings and records of the lives of the philosophers, many of whom were ancient to him already. But the story was remembered for a reason. It captures the essential convictions of the Stoics.

They believed that life was grounded in a benign principle they called the *logos*. *Logos* is one of those Greek words that can be translated in numerous ways, as word or reason, discourse or principle, law or activity, allure or attraction. The earliest extended Stoic text to survive the centuries is a hymn to Zeus, penned by Cleanthes, the second head of the Stoic school. He praises the high god for the *logos* that 'moves through all creation'. He celebrates it as the wellspring of unity, direction, meaning, purpose. Suffering, he argues, arises from refusing the *logos*. Ignorance of its workings leads men and women into all manner of false hopes and expectations – the pursuit of fame and fortune, of pleasure for pleasure's sake, that is Epicureanism, we might infer. But troubles resolve themselves in the letting go inherent in learning to follow the *logos*.

Their training was an attempt, gradually, to orient the whole of your life to its deep, barely perceptible ways. Stoics strove to 'go with the flow', one of their phrases, to become aware of their own humdrum, persistent anxieties and concerns so as to not be bound by them. To borrow an analogy from Chrysippus, the third head of the school: consider a cylinder rolling down a hill. Life is like that. Once it gets going, it will take you in this downward direction regardless of how you resist. Your freedom, therefore, lies in embracing the knocks and blows, trusting that all ends well in the valley. Suffering arises from hating and bemoaning and cursing and fearing the knocks and blows. Though it's far easier to say than do, the Stoics argued that there is another way.

Recognition of the *logos* was another response to Socrates. Life often feels bewildering and unsettling in the way Socrates showed us, the Stoics suggested, that is true. But it is because we lose touch with this source or ground, 'in whom we live and move and have our being,' as they put it. Beneath our uncertainties a divine providence guides all things.

It was not an entirely original interpolation. Many ancient people sensed that life had direction, was directed by fate. The Stoics added that you could trust it. 'You are a fragment of God,' they said. 'You are never alone.' The basic lesson in life is that there is a God. And it is rational to sing the divine praises because God is good. All things turn out for the best, regardless of how they might seem to you. To live in accordance with this divine aspect of nature is to find your self-sufficiency. Look at Zeno's own life. It demonstrated as much.

You could not discern this immanent pattern and pulse overnight, let alone live by it. The Stoics' metaphysics was intimately connnected to the way of life that led them gradually to know of the *logos* in the depths of their souls. They developed a variety of practices and techniques for opening yourself up to its operation, for shifting your worldview. Many of them are collected in a text called the *Handbook*, the sayings of a Stoic of the first and second centuries CE, Epictetus.

Incidentally, life did not look promising for Epictetus at first, either. He was born a slave and crippled. His name means 'acquired'. But his wisdom became highly valued. First Stoics and then early Christians deployed his methods as they trained themselves to live well by this philosophy. The *Handbook* survives to our day because it was so frequently copied.

You can try Epictetus-like tests on yourself because following Zeno in the *stoa*, he felt that the small incidents of everyday life provide the best material with which to train yourself to embrace life's hardships, to notice how you respond to what happens. If you wait until a crisis – a death or divorce or disaster – then it'll probably be too late for Stoicism to help. So next time you are driving and another car cuts you up, ask yourself how you felt. With what emotion did you respond? Anger? Fright? Retaliatory aggression? It's an ideal moment to practice a key insight for Epictetus, namely that it is not what happens to us that causes us problems, but how we respond to what happens. If you do not erupt in road rage but keep your calm, being cut up probably doesn't matter. Become more conscious of such reactions and the deeper patterns of life might become perceptible too. Instead of being caught in the turbulent web of your own emotion, you may come to see the truth about the way the cosmos flows, about the divine presence in nature.

The idea that it is how we react to events that troubles us, not the events in themselves, has become a commonplace in books of self-help and advice. More systematically, it has been developed into the methods of Cognitive Behavioural Therapy. The founders of CBT were self-consciously Stoic, arguing that the techniques of Zeno and his followers can be used, though without needing to believe in the *logos* or God.

Certainly, there is evidence that CBT does help people escape from the prisons of anxiety or depression. What is unclear is how long the benefits last. Now that longitudinal studies of CBT are being published, counted in years rather than months, it seems to be the case that CBT can offer invaluable help out of a deep rut, but then a little further down the line, many individuals begin to feel themselves becoming trapped again.

I suspect that part of the issue here is that prizing apart Stoic practices from the logos-centric worldview undermines the philosophy's *raison d'être*. It leaves the cognitive method uprooted from felt foundations. The difficulty is that the most common and scientifically 'official' philosophical stance today is that the cosmos is not benign. It is indifferent. Science, for the most part, works on the assumption that nature is mechanical, no more purposeful than a car crash or a Mediterranean storm. Neither is the cosmos to be trusted with your life. In fact, much of the modern economy and our own personal energies are geared towards resisting and fighting what can happen to us, to preserving our happiness in spite of happenstance. The double difficulty is that much good is achieved in this process too.

The ancient Stoics were not passive in the face of suffering. Much as they argued against the Cynics that many social conventions are neither good nor bad, and so can be embraced, so too pain need not be masochistically endured if cures were known or could be found. But the deeper sense of trusting life is crucial for the way of life they advocated to bed down. If a sense of the divine is written off ahead of time, the techniques remain just that: techniques. They don't root the individual in a source of life bigger than their own. Further, if nature is blind as science usually teaches, it may be more rational to rail at fate, to become angry when things go wrong, to kick against the goad, not go with the flow.

Personally, I'm inclined to feel that CBT and related schools of advice conceal a philosophical void and therefore a therapeutic flaw. But another group of ancient Jews and Romans adopted much from Stoic philosophy including a renewed sense of the *logos*. Their experience developed into another way of life, one that thrives to this day. They were the early Christians. Individuals like St Paul and the writer of the gospel of John tried to understand what the life, death and resurrection of Jesus of Nazareth meant to them. Stoicism offered rich resources. Perhaps, Paul mused and then taught, Jesus revealed the God in whom the Stoics felt they lived and moved and had their being. The New Testament tells of Paul going to Athens and arguing as much with the Stoics. Some laughed at him. Some followed him.

Or maybe Jesus was the *logos* incarnate, John's gospel proposes, in its opening lines: 'The word [*logos*] was made flesh and dwelt among us, full of grace and truth.' This is a radical twist to the Stoicism Zeno taught. How could the benign *logos* suffer the crucified's fate, he might have asked? How can suffering be not something from which to seek escape, but something that itself leads us into a deeper perception of God? But it made sense to some, then to more, then to many.

Christianity drew much from Platonism too, particularly in its understanding that wisdom comes via the way of love. But again, there were differences and developments. Plato held to love of the beautiful, good and true, not the kind of love that offers itself on a cross. It is the Jewish side of Christianity that supplies such insights, as well as the notion that God might act definitively in the lives of special human beings, and through what happens in history change the course of history.

For a few centuries after what some claimed to be the death and resurrection of the *logos*, Stoics and Platonists, as well as the other followers of Socrates, existed side by side – sometimes angrily; often interacting as high-minded friends. Gradually, Christianity came to dominate, at least in the west. But whilst this story is often told now as one of domination, it was also a handing on of the baton, a remaking of the ancient Greek philosophies, now centuries old. A nice coincidence of history captures the exchange. In 529CE, Plato's Academy was finally closed in Athens. With interruptions, it had existed for 900 years. But in the same year, St Benedict opened his monastery at Monte Cassino. These new philosophers were called monks not sages. They wrote what we now call theology not philosophy. But they spoke out of a dedicated way of life. They disciplined and trained themselves. They realised that the central issue is to shift your perception of life, of what exists and what is true. They were followers of Jesus, but still of Socrates too.

APPENDIX I

The Schools of Ancient Philosophy in one minute

Plato – Platonism

Key fact: The star pupil of Socrates.
Must have: A love of the biggest speculative questions in life.
Key promise: The contemplation of eternity.
Key peril: His philosophy is thought by some to be pseudo-religious nonsense.
Most likely to say: 'There are more things in heaven and earth than can even be dreamt by philosophy.'
Least likely to say: 'Get real! Life has no meaning.'
Text to try: His dialogue, the *Symposium*.

Aristotle – the Peripatetics

Key fact: The star pupil of Plato.
Must have: A desire to study the world and see what it reveals.
Key promise: The good life, which comes from living virtuously.
Key peril: The virtuous life is not always a pleasurable life.
Most likely to say: 'Everything has its proper place.'
Least likely to say: 'Science is where humanity went wrong.'
Text to try: Books VIII & IX of his *Nicomachean Ethics*, on friendship.

Zeno – the Stoics

Key fact: He taught in a stoa, the Athenian market, and hence founded the school of philosophy called Stoicism.

Must have: An interest in the humdrum, for it is in everyday life that you learn best how to live.

Key promise: An ability to face anything, no matter how disastrous.

Key peril: To think 'stoical' is to give up your passions.

Most likely to say: 'If you have integrity, no-one can harm you.'

Least likely to say: 'Forget prudence! It won't help you anyway.'

Text to try: Seneca's essays – the Roman philosopher who was a Stoic.

Epicurus – the Epicureans

Key fact: Epicurus, founder of Epicureanism, is the ancient world's hedonist, though he recommended quality not quantity when it came to the pursuit of pleasure.

Must have: A delight in the countryside and gardens.

Key promise: Tranquillity born of happiness in small things.

Key peril: Boredom.

Most likely to say: 'The true hedonist can find as much pleasure in a glass of chilled water as a feast for a king.'

Least likely to say: 'He who tires of the city, tires of life.'

Text to try: His surviving maxims and letters are very readable and collected in a number of modern translations.

Pyrrho – the Sceptics

Key fact: Pyrrho is traditionally known as the founder of the Sceptical tradition of philosophy.

Must have: Patience with yourself.

Key promise: Tranquillity born of letting things be.

Key peril: It's hard to let things be.

Most likely to say: 'Don't worry: be happy.'

Least likely to say: 'There is an answer to everything.'

Text to try: Pyrrho left no books. However, the readable essays of Michel de Montaigne are much inspired by him.

Diogenes – the Cynics

Key fact: Diogenes was called a cynic, from the Greek for 'dog', because some said he lived like a dog.

Must have: A love of going *au naturel*. (He famously had sex in public.)

Key promise: Not a care in the world.

Key peril: This way of life upset lots of people.

Most likely to say: 'A barrel is as good an abode as a house.'

Least likely to say: 'Happiness is found by being conventional.'

Text to try: Diogenes wrote nothing. However, look up his name in any biography of Alexander the Great, and you'll find out about his most famous encounter.

APPENDIX 2

Some key dates

469 BCE	Socrates born, Aeschylus writes tragedies
424/8	Plato born
431	Peloponnesian War begins
c412	Diogenes the Cynic born
406	Euripides and Sophocles die
c405	Plato meets Socrates
404	Peloponnesian War ends
399	Socrates executed
c387	Plato founds the Academy in Athens
c385	Plato writes the *Symposium*
384	Aristotle born
367	Aristotle joins Plato's Academy
365	Pyrrho of Elis, the Sceptic, born
347	Plato dies, Aristotle leaves Athens
341	Epicurus born
c338	Aristotle becomes tutor to Alexander the Great
c335	Aristotle founds the Lyceum in Athens
334	Zeno of Citium, the Stoic, born

323	Diogenes the Cynic dies
322	Aristotle dies in exile
306	Epicurus returns to Athens and founds the Garden
300	Zeno of Citium beings teaching in the Painted Stoa
275	Pyrrho of Elis dies
270	Epicurus dies
262	Death of Zeno
155 BCE	Diogenes of Babylon introduces the Romans to Stoicism …

APPENDIX 3

Further reading and listening

Some primary sources to try:

Aristotle, *Nichomachean Ethics*, Books VIII-X, translated by Sarah Broadie and Christopher Rowe (Oxford University Press)

Barnes, Jonathan (ed), *Early Greek Philosophy – Pre-Socratics* (Penguin Classics)

Epicurus Reader, edited by Brad Inwood, L. P. Gerson and D. S. Hutchinson (Hackett)

Epictetus, *The Handbook* (Several publishers, though try the Hackett edition)

Plato, *Symposium*, translated by Alexander Nehamas and Paul Woodruff (Hackett)

Seneca, *Dialogues and Letters* (Penguin Classics)

Some secondary material:

Annas, Julia, *Ancient Philosophy: A Very Short Introduction* (Oxford University Press)

Osborne, Catherine, *Presocratic Philosophy: A Very Short Introduction* (OUP)

– Other books in this series, on particular philosophers, are very helpful too

Kenny, Anthony, *A New History of Western Philosophy*, Volume 1: Ancient Philosophy (Clarendon Press)

Sellars, John, *Stoicism* (Acumen – in its excellent Ancient Philosophy series, which has books on all the ancient schools)

O'Keefe, Tim, *Epicureanism*, (the Acumen series again)

Other more general reading:

Evans, Jules, *Philosophy for Life and Other Dangerous Situations* (Rider)

Gottlieb, Anthony, *The Dream of Reason* (Penguin)

Vernon, Mark, *Plato's Podcasts: The Ancient's Guide to Modern Living* (Oneworld)

Podcasts:

The History of Philosophy Without Any Gaps with Peter Adamson, http://www.historyofphilosophy.net

In Our Time with Melvyn Bragg, BBC Radio 4 programme http://www.bbc.co.uk/prgrammes/b006qykl
Episodes to date have included Heraclitus, Pythagoras, Socrates, The School of Athens, Aristotle's Poetics, Aristotle's Politics, Cynicism, Stoicism, Plato's Symposium, and others

Plato's Podcasts, short films on Youtube with Mark Vernon http://www.youtube.com/user/PlatosPodcasts

Aristotle's philosophy of friendship with Mark Vernon http://itunes.apple.com/gb/podcast/aristotles-philosophy-friendship/id170142977

Acknowledgments

My thanks go to Tom Hodgkinson for publishing the book, and to Victoria Hull too, for their vision and support with the classes at The Idler Academy upon which the text is based. I am indebted to John Sellars and Patrick Ussher for reading the manuscript, putting up with my swipes at academic philosophy, and still being prepared to offer helpful corrections. Thanks as well to Christian Brett & Alice Smith for ensuring the book looks fine.